For Laurel and Shanti,
with much love
from Reeve

For Paul, Louisa,
and William,
with love, Cathie

First published 1998 by Walker Books Ltd
87 Vauxhall Walk, London SE11 5HJ

10 9 8 7 6 5 4 3 2 1

Text © 1998 Reeve Lindbergh
Illustrations © 1998 Cathie Felstead

This book has been typeset in Leawood Book.

Printed in Italy

British Library Cataloguing in Publication Data
A catalogue record for this book is
available from the British Library.

ISBN 0-7445-4047-X

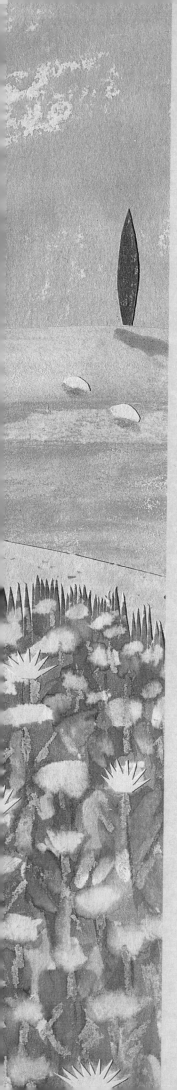

Reeve Lindbergh

The Circle of Days

From *Canticle of the Sun* by Saint Francis of Assisi

Saint Francis of Assisi (1182-1226) lived in Italy, where he founded the Franciscan order of monks. He is one of the world's best-loved saints, known for his devotion to nature, especially animals and birds. His *Canticle of the Sun,* written in 1225, has been translated into many languages and has been adapted in poetry and song throughout the centuries, as a hymn of praise.

illustrated by

Cathie Felstead

WALKER BOOKS
AND SUBSIDIARIES
LONDON • BOSTON • SYDNEY

Lord, we offer thanks and praise
For the circle of our days.
Praise for radiant brother sun,
Who makes the hours around us run.

For sister moon, and for the stars,

Brilliant, precious, always ours.

Praise for brothers wind and air,

Serene or cloudy, foul or fair.

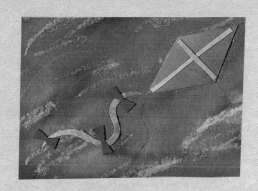

For sister water, clear and chaste,

Useful, humble, good to taste.

For fire, our brother, strong and bright,

Whose joy illuminates the night.

Praise for our sister, mother earth,

Who cares for each of us from birth.

For all her children, fierce or mild,

For sister, brother, parent, child.

For creatures wild, and creatures tame,

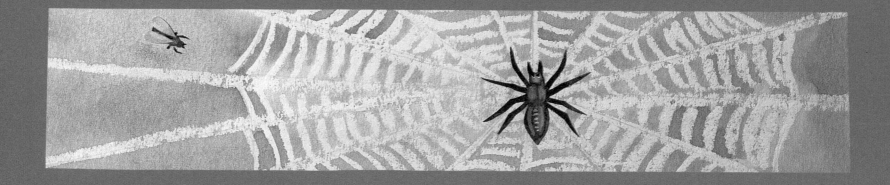

For hunter, hunted, both the same.

For brother sleep, and sister death,

Who tend the borders of our breath.

For desert, orchard, rock, and tree,

For forest, meadow, mountain, sea,

For fruit and flower, plant and bush,

For morning robin, evening thrush.

For all your gifts, of every kind,
We offer praise with quiet mind.
Be with us, Lord, and guide our ways
Around the circle of our days.